MW00990958

MASTER THEORY

Elementary Harmony & Arranging Workbook

by Charles S. Peters and Paul Yoder

The Fourth Workbook in the MASTER THEORY SERIES

CONTENTS

ISBN 0-8497-0157-0

Lesson 1

TRIADS

A TRIAD is a chord of three tones consisting of a root, third and fifth.

Triads in both treble and bass clef:

The ROOT is the tone on which a triad is built. When the root appears as the lowest tone, the triad is said to be in ROOT POSITION.

A MAJOR TRIAD is a chord of three tones consisting of a root, major third and perfect fifth.

Major triads in root position:

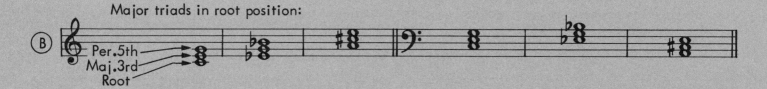

The triad built on the first degree of the scale is called a TONIC TRIAD. It is marked with a Roman numeral I below and a capital letter for the name of the chord (triad) above.

In any major scale the tonic triad is a MAJOR CHORD.

The triad built on the fifth degree of the scale is called a DOMINANT TRIAD. It is marked with a Roman numeral V below and a capital letter for the name of the chord (triad) above.

In any major scale the dominant triad is a MAJOR CHORD.

Tonic and dominant triads in major keys:

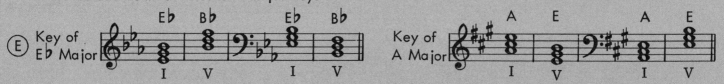

* For review of triads, see MASTER THEORY—Book 3, Lessons 83–88.

STUDENT ASSIGNMENT

Date _____

Grade _____

In Ex. 1 and 2 write the major chords I and V above the Roman numerals in the keys indicated. Write the letter names of the chords above.

In Ex. 3 and 4 write the major chords below their letter names in the keys indicated. Write the proper Roman numerals below.

In Ex. 5 and 6 fill in the missing note in the major chords and write the letter name of the chord above. All chords are to be in root position.

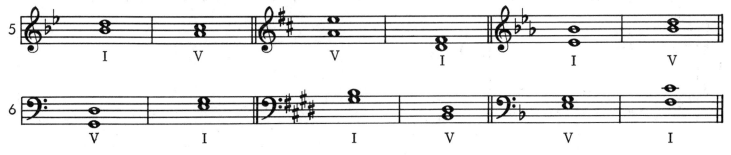

In Ex. 7 and 8 write the proper Roman numerals under each chord and the letter names above.

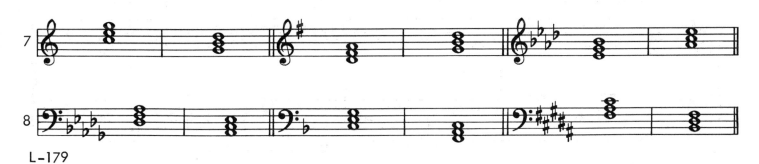

Lesson 3
HARMONIZING WITH CHORDS

The following melody can be harmonized with only two chords; the TONIC, built on the first degree of the scale and the DOMINANT, built on the fifth degree of the scale. The melody is based entirely on the tones of these two chords. Dashes denote the duration of each chord.

This is the same melody in another key with the tune in the bass clef and the chords in the treble clef.

Lesson 4

STUDENT ASSIGNMENT

Date _____

Grade _____

Transpose the melody from (A) on page 4 in the treble clef, to the key of G and harmonize with chords in the bass clef. Write the Roman numerals below the chords in the bass clef and the letter names of the chords above the melody in the treble clef. Extend dashes for the duration of each chord.

Transpose the melody from (B) on page 4 in the bass clef, to the key of B♭ and harmonize with chords in the treble clef. Write the Roman numerals below the melody in the bass clef and the letter names of the chords above in the treble clef. Extend dashes for the duration of each chord.

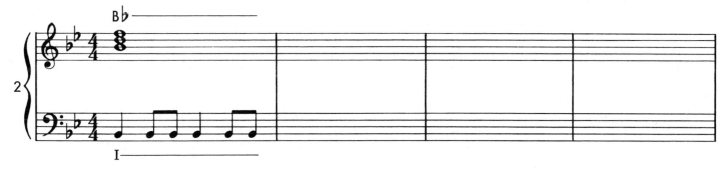

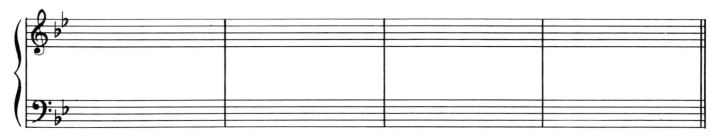

L-179

Lesson 5

PASSING AND NEIGHBORING NOTES

This is a melody in which some of the notes are not contained in the triad used for the harmonic background. Such notes are either PASSING NOTES or NEIGHBORING NOTES. Passing notes are those notes that lie between chord notes and are not part of the chord. They are marked with a (P). A neighboring note is a note lying a half tone or a whole tone above or below the chord note. It returns to the original chord note. Neighboring notes are marked with an (N).

Here is a melody in which some of the notes are not contained in the chords that are used as harmonic background. In this case, both the E and the G in the third measure would be called PASSING NOTES. The chord is sustained in the harmonic background while the melody passes thru these non-chordal notes.

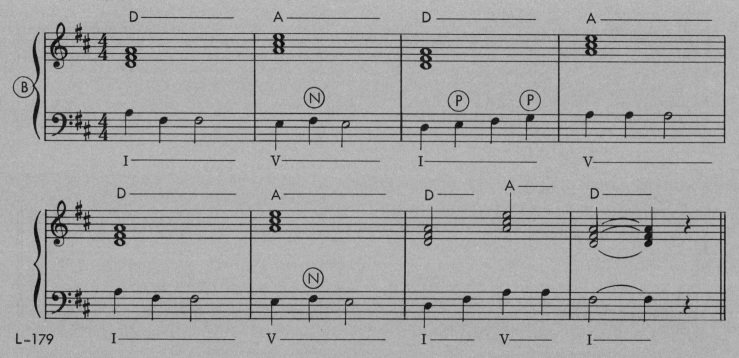

STUDENT ASSIGNMENT

Date _____

Grade _____

Transpose the melody Ⓐ on page 6 to the bass clef, in the key of F major and harmonize with chords in the treble clef. Write the Roman numerals below the melodic line in the bass clef and the letter names of the chords above in the treble clef. Mark the passing (P) or neighboring (N) notes.

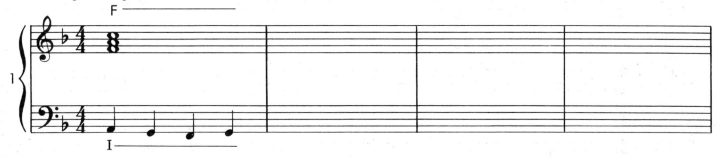

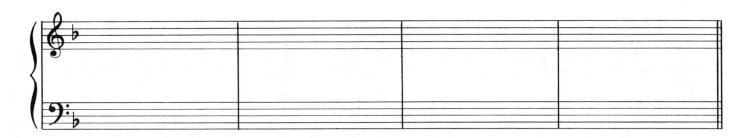

Transpose the melody from Ⓑ on page 6 to the treble clef, in the key of G and harmonize with chords in the bass clef. Write the Roman numerals below the chords in the bass clef and the letter names of the chords above the melody line in the treble clef. Mark the passing (P) or neighboring (N) notes.

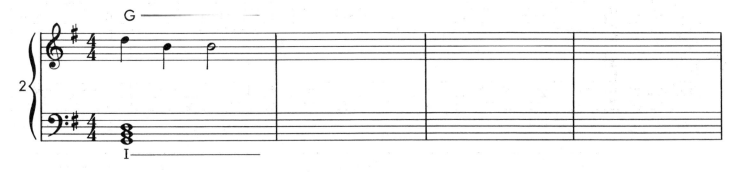

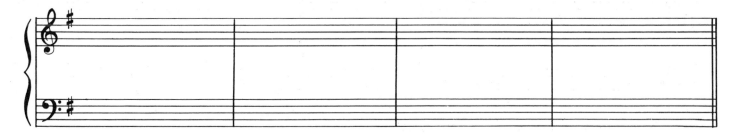

Lesson 7

TRIADS IN ARPEGGIO FORM

An ARPEGGIO is a broken chord in which the tones are played successively, one after another. It is often used in writing an accompaniment for a melody.*

*Here is another melody with an accompaniment in arpeggio form.

N = neighboring note; P = passing note.

* Play both melodies on the piano.

STUDENT ASSIGNMENT

Date _____

Grade _____

Transpose the melody from (A) on page 8 in the treble clef, to the key of Eb with the arpeggio accompaniment in the bass clef. Write the Roman numerals and letter names of the chords in their places. Mark the passing (P) or neighboring (N) notes.

Transpose the melody (B) on page 8 in the treble clef, to the key of D with the arpeggio accompaniment in the bass clef. Write the Roman numerals and letter names of the chords in their proper places. Mark the passing (P) or neighboring (N) notes.

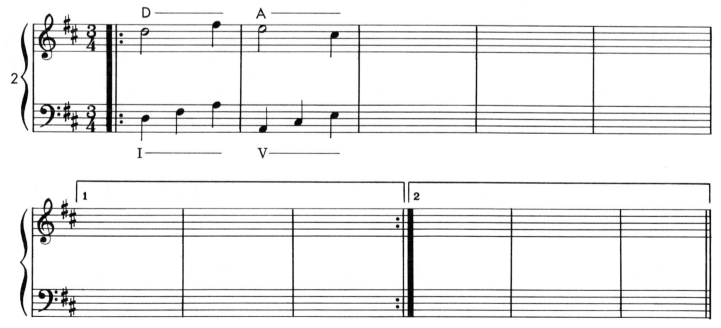

Lesson 9
THE SUBDOMINANT TRIAD

The triad built on the fourth degree of the scale is called the SUBDOMINANT. It is marked with a Roman numeral IV below and a capital letter for the name of the chord above. In any major scale the subdominant triad is a major chord.

The TONIC (I), SUBDOMINANT (IV), and DOMINANT (V) TRIADS are known as the PRINCIPAL CHORDS in any key.

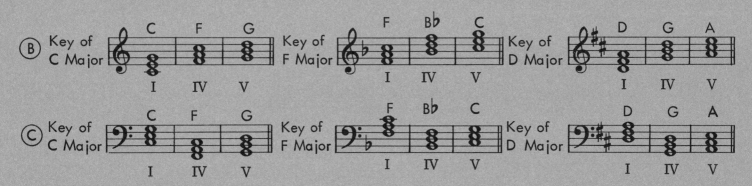

This melody is harmonized with the three principal chords in root position.

The same melody written with an accompaniment in arpeggio form.

(P) = passing note.

STUDENT ASSIGNMENT

In Ex. 1 and 2 write the principal chords in triad form in the indicated major keys. Watch the clef sign carefully. Write the letter name of each chord above.

In Ex. 3 and 4 write these same chords as they would appear in arpeggio form. Watch the clef sign carefully. Write the letter name of each chord above.

Transpose the melody from Ⓓ on page 10 in the treble clef to the key of E♭, with the proper chords in the bass clef. Write the Roman numerals and letter names of the chords.

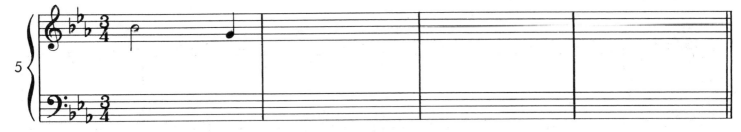

Transpose this same melody in the treble clef to the key of A with an arpeggio accompaniment in the style of Ⓔ on page 10. Write the Roman numerals and letter names of the chords.

L-179

Lesson 11

THE DOMINANT SEVENTH CHORD

A DOMINANT SEVENTH CHORD consists of a root, major 3rd, perfect 5th, and minor 7th. It usually moves to the tonic or I chord. It is marked V7 and the 7 is added to the letter name, such as G7 or C7.

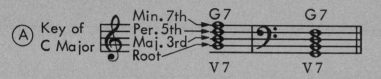
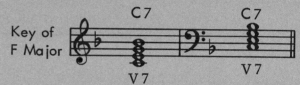

The following melody is harmonized with I-IV-V7 chords.

The same melody with an arpeggio accompaniment. Note the addition of the octave to the tonic and subdominant triads.

Lesson 12

STUDENT ASSIGNMENT

Date _____

Grade _____

Write the dominant seventh chord in the keys indicated and write the letter name of the chord above. Watch the clef sign.

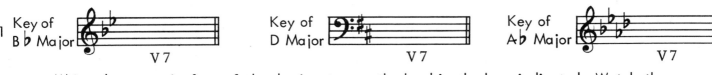

Write the arpeggio form of the dominant seventh chord in the keys indicated. Watch the clef sign.

Write the harmonic progression as indicated in whole notes and write the letter name above each chord.

Write the same progression in arpeggio form using quarter notes and write the letter name above each chord.

Transpose the melody from page 12 in the treble clef to the key of A♭. Write an arpeggio accompaniment in the bass clef. Write the Roman numerals and letter names of the chords.

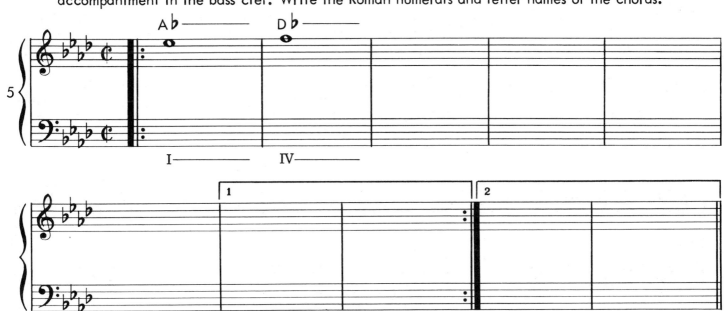

L-179

Lesson 13

MELODY WRITING

In the next three lessons we will present ideas which will help you to write melodies.

The following original melody uses only the notes of the chords; no passing or neighboring notes. Note: we start and end with the I chord.

Melody (B) uses a different arrangement of the chords. Note: this melody also starts and ends with the I chord. All notes in the melody are contained in the chords.

Lesson 14

STUDENT ASSIGNMENT

Date _____

Grade _____

In Ex. 1 and 2 write an original melody in the treble clef in the keys indicated using only the notes of the chords; no passing or neighboring notes.

Note the variation of the chord notes used in the arpeggio accompaniment.

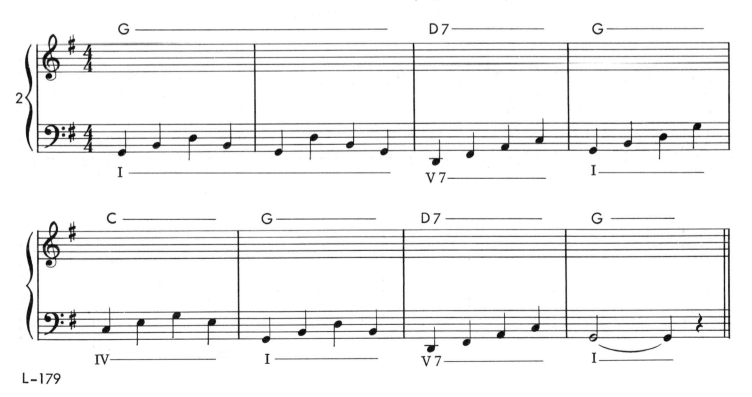

L-179

Lesson 15

MELODY WRITING

The following original melody uses notes contained in the chords plus passing (P) notes and neighboring (N) notes. We start and end with the I (tonic) chord.

This familiar melody uses passing (P) notes and neighboring (N) notes.

HICKORY DICKORY DOCK

STUDENT ASSIGNMENT

Date _____

Grade _____

In Ex. 1 and 2 write an original melody in the treble clef, in the keys indicated, using notes of the chords plus passing and neighboring notes. Complete the bass clef chords in arpeggio form first. Mark the passing (P) and neighboring (N) notes.

Lesson 17

MELODY WRITING

The following examples illustrate three different melodies written to the same harmonic progression. A note from the harmony chord is used on the first beat of each measure.

Lesson 18
STUDENT ASSIGNMENT

Date _____

Grade _____

Write two different, original melodies in the treble clef, in the key of F. Begin each measure with a note from the harmony chord. Mark the passing (P) and neighboring (N) notes.

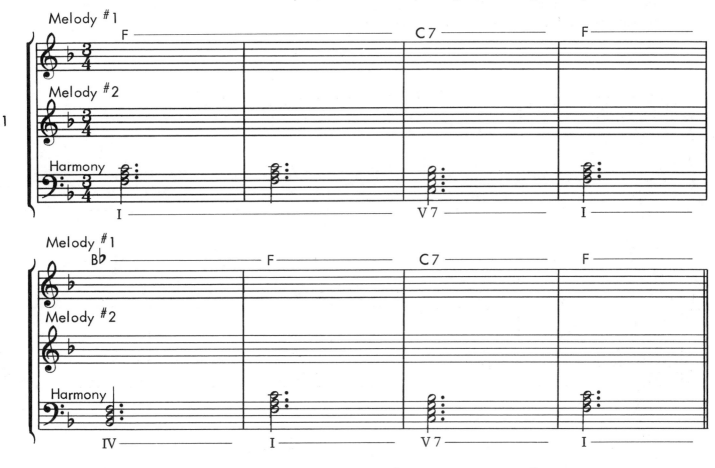

Complete the following melody. Mark the passing (P) and neighboring (N) notes.

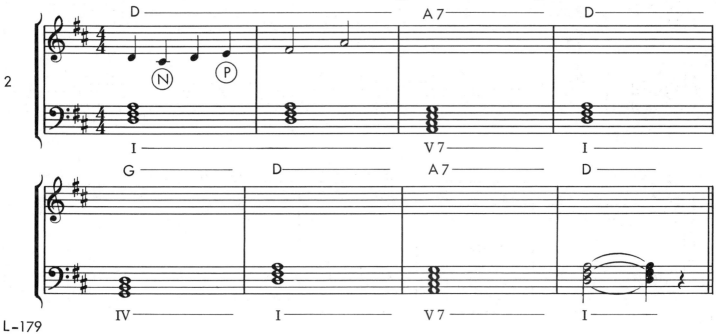

Lesson 19

HARMONIZING A MELODY

The I-IV-V-V7 chords are the most important ones which we use in harmonizing a melody. Since the three major chords I, IV, and V contain every note of the major scale, we can harmonize most simple melodies with these chords. Note: we usually begin and end a melody with a I chord and a V or V7 chord usually occurs before the I chord at the end. Study the chords used to harmonize the familiar melodies in Ex. Ⓐ and Ⓑ.

GOOD NIGHT, LADIES

WHERE HAS MY LITTLE DOG GONE?

Lesson 20

STUDENT ASSIGNMENT

Date	_____
Grade	_____

Harmonize melodies 1 and 2 using I-IV-V-V7 chords only. Remember, we usually begin and end a melody with a I chord, and a V or V7 chord usually occurs before the I chord at the end. Write the letter names of the chords above the treble clef staff and the Roman numerals below the bass clef staff.

WHISPERING WALTZ

Lesson 21

REVIEW

Date _____

Grade _____

In Ex. 1 and 2, write the I–IV–V7 chords in whole notes, in the major keys indicated, and write their letter names above the chords. Watch the clef signs.

In Ex. 3 and 4, write the I–IV–V7 chords in arpeggio form, in the major keys indicated. Use quarter notes. Watch the clef sign. Write the letter names above the chords.

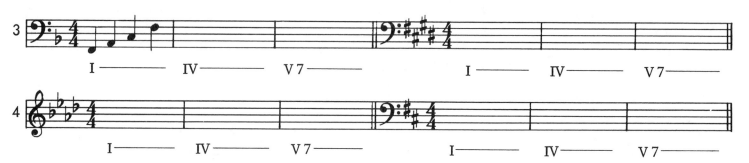

Write an original melody in the treble clef, in the key of G, to fit the chord progression in the bass clef. Write the letter names above the treble clef staff. Mark the passing Ⓟ and neighboring Ⓝ notes.

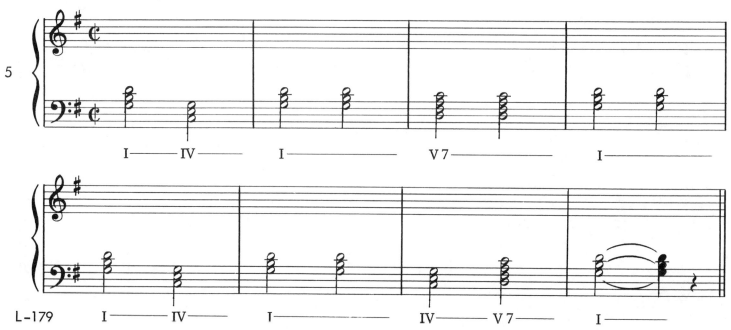

L-179

Lesson 22

REVIEW

Date _____

Grade _____

In Ex. 1, using half notes, write the chords in the bass clef which are indicated by the letter names above the melody. Write the proper Roman numerals below the bass clef staff.

In Ex. 2 use the arpeggio form for writing the harmony part, using I-IV-V-V7 chords only. Mark the chord letter names above the treble clef staff and the Roman numerals below the bass clef staff.

L-179

Lesson 23

I-IV-V⁷ IN MINOR

Harmonic accompaniments in minor keys are usually based on the harmonic minor scale.

(A) The harmonic minor scale begins on the 6th degree of its relative major scale and ascends or descends for one octave using the key signature of the major scale except that the 7th tone is raised 1/2 step. (See arrow in the example below) Notice that the 3rd tone of the minor scale is only 1/2 step from the 2nd. This is the most characteristic feature of minor scales.

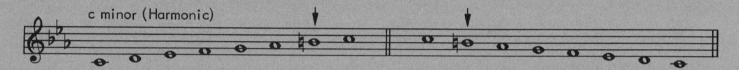

(B) A minor triad is a chord of three tones consisting of a root – minor third – and perfect fifth. In any harmonic minor scale the triads built on the tonic (I) and subdominant (IV) are minor chords. Minor chords are marked with a small letter (a – f – g – etc.).

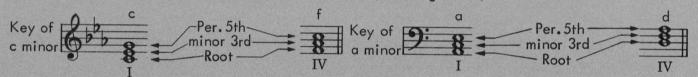

(C) In any harmonic minor scale the triad built on the dominant (V) is a major chord. The raised 7th tone of the harmonic minor scale becomes the major 3rd of the V or V7 chord.

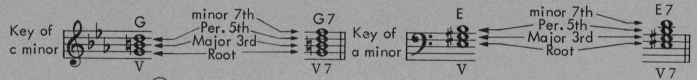

(D) The melody in Ex.(D) is in the key of a minor and is harmonized with I-IV-V 7 chords. Note that the I and IV chords are both minor (minor 3rd) but the V7 chord contains a major 3rd.

Lesson 24

STUDENT ASSIGNMENT

Date _____

Grade _____

In Ex. 1 and 2 write the harmonic minor scale, ascending and descending in the indicated keys.

Key of e minor

Key of d minor

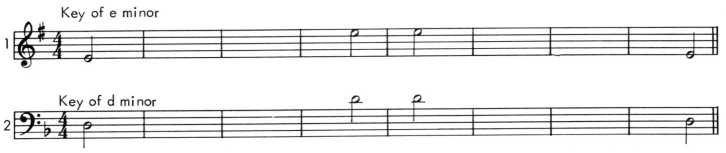

In Ex. 3 and 4 write I, IV, and V7 in whole notes, in the minor keys indicated. Mark the letter names above the chords using small letters for minor triads. Remember the raised seventh degree of the harmonic minor scale which becomes the major third of the chord in V7.

Transpose the melody from Ⓓ on page 24 in the treble clef, to the key of f minor and harmonize with I, IV, and V7 chords. Write the Roman numerals below the bass clef staff and letter names above the treble clef staff.

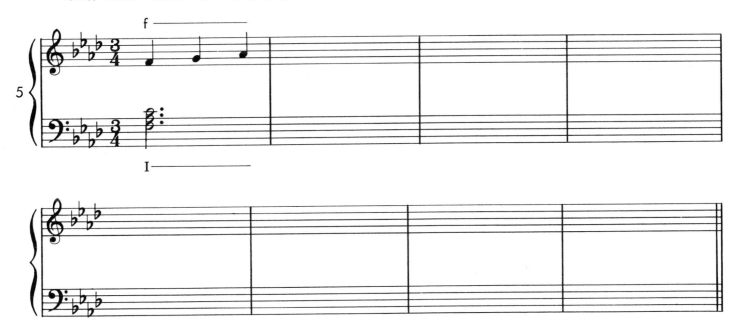

L-179

Lesson 25

RECOGNIZING MAJOR CHORDS

Date _____

Grade _____

In Ex. (A) circle all major I (tonic) chords.

In Ex. (B) circle all major IV (subdominant) chords.

SILENT NIGHT

In Ex. (C) circle all V7 (dominant seventh) chords.

CIELITO LINDO

RECOGNIZING MINOR CHORDS

Date _____

Grade _____

In Ex. (A) circle all minor I (tonic) chords.

RUSSIAN FOLK SONG

In Ex. (B) circle all minor IV (subdominant) chords.

In Ex. (C) circle all the V 7 (dominant seventh) chords. Notice that this melody does not begin on the I (tonic) chord.

DANUBE WAVES

Lesson 27

REVIEW

Date _____

Grade _____

In Ex. 1 and 2 write the I-IV-V 7 in whole note chords in the minor keys indicated. Watch the clef signs. Write the letter names above the chords.

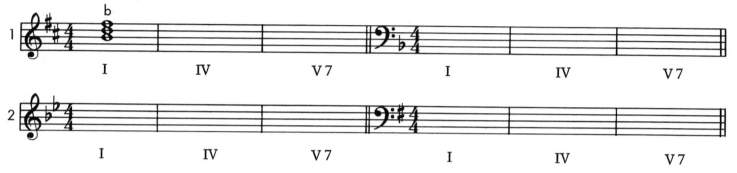

In Ex. 3 and 4 write the I-IV-V 7 in arpeggio form in the minor keys indicated. Use quarter notes . Watch the clef signs. Write the letter names above the chords.

Write an original melody in the treble clef in the key of g minor to fit the chord progression in the bass clef. Write the letter names of the chords above the treble clef staff. Mark the passing Ⓟ and neighboring Ⓝ notes.

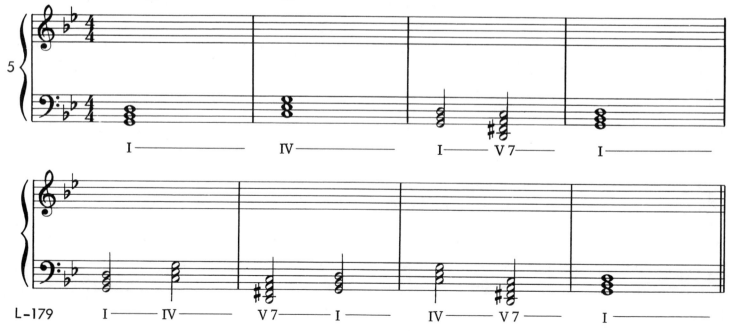

L-179

Lesson 28

REVIEW

Date _____

Grade _____

In Ex. Ⓐ circle all V7 (dominant seventh) chords. Mark all passing (P) and neighboring (N) notes.

BELIEVE ME IF ALL THOSE ENDEARING YOUNG CHARMS

In Ex. Ⓑ circle all minor I (tonic) chords. Mark all passing (P) and neighboring (N) notes. This melody does not begin on the I (tonic) chord.

LA CUMPARSITA

Lesson 29
STUDENT TEST

Date _____

Grade _____

Lesson 1   1. A triad is a chord of _____ tones consisting of a _____ ,

_____ , and _____ .

2. When the root appears as the lowest tone, the triad is said to be in _____ _____ .

3. A major triad is a chord of _____ tones consisting of a _____ ,

_____ _____ , and _____ _____ .

4. Write the Roman numerals below and the letter names above the following major triads.

Lesson 3   1. Using whole notes, write the proper triads below the following melody. Mark the Roman numerals and letter names.

Lesson 5   1. Mark the passing Ⓟ and neighboring Ⓝ notes in the following melody.

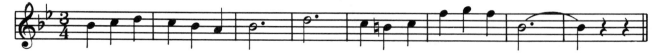

Lesson 7   1. Write the major triads indicated below in arpeggio form.

Lesson 9   1. The names of the principal chords in any key are the _____ ,

_____ , and _____ .

2. Using whole notes, write the triads I-IV-V in the following major keys.

Lesson 30

STUDENT TEST

Date _____
Grade _____

Lesson 11 1. The dominant seventh is a chord of _____ tones consisting of a _____ ,
_____ _____ , _____ _____ , and _____ _____ .

2. Using whole notes, write the progression I-IV-V7 in these major keys. Watch the clef signs.

3. Write the arpeggio form of the dominant seventh chord (V7) in the indicated major keys.

Lesson 13 1. Write an original melody in the treble clef in the key indicated, using only the notes of the chords—no passing (P) or neighboring (N) notes. Write the letter names of the chords above your melody.

Lesson 15 1. Write an original melody in the treble clef in the key indicated, using notes of the chords plus passing (P) and neighboring (N) notes. Write the letter names of the chords above your melody.

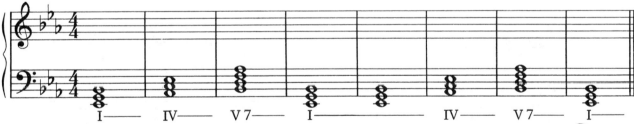

Lesson 17 1. Write an original melody in the treble clef in the key indicated. Mark the passing (P) and neighboring (N) notes.

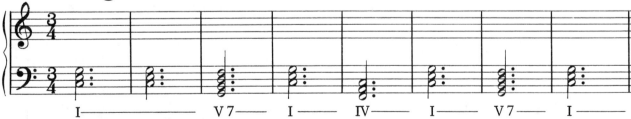

Lesson 19 1. Using half notes, harmonize the following melody with I-IV-V7 chords only. Mark the Roman numerals below the bass clef staff and the letter names of the chords above the melody.

L-179

Lesson 30 (continued)

STUDENT TEST

Date _____
Grade _____

Lesson 23 **1.** A minor triad is a chord of _____ tones consisting of _____ ,

_____ , and _____ .

2. Using whole notes, write the progression I-IV-V 7 in the following minor keys. Watch the clef signs. Remember the accidental in the V 7 chord.

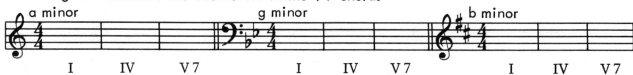

3. In all major and minor keys, the dominant (V) and dominant seventh (V 7) chords always contain a _____ third.

4. Write the arpeggio form of the dominant seventh (V 7) in the following minor keys. Watch the clef signs. Remember the accidental on the major third.

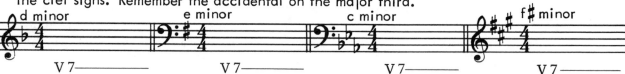

Lesson 25 **1.** The following melody is written in the key of _____ . Write the Roman numerals and letter names for all chords. Mark passing (P) and neighboring (N) notes.

MARINE'S HYMN

Lesson 26 **1.** The following melody is written in the key of _____ . Write the Roman numerals and letter names for all chords. Mark passing (P) and neighboring (N) notes.